THE ANTOINE DUPONT STORY

How One of France's Finest Evolved to Becoming a European Rugby Living Legend

The Sport Haven

The Antoine Dupont Story

Copyright © 2024 by The Sport Haven

All rights reserved. No part of this publication may be reproduced, distributed, or transmitted in any form or by any means, including photocopying, recording, or other electronic or mechanical methods, without the prior written permission of the publisher, except in the case of brief quotations embodied in critical reviews and certain other non-commercial uses permitted by copyright law.

The Sport Haven

The Antoine Dupont Story

Dear Esteemed Rugby Fan,

Thank you so much for your recent purchase of the book. I do hope you have been able to learn a few or two about your favorite Rugby star. Your support means the world to us, and we're thrilled to have you here. We hope that the pages within provide you with inspiration, creativity and knowledge to being the best at whatsoever athletic endeavor you chose to delve into.

As sports enthusiasts, your enthusiasm fuels our passion, and we are genuinely grateful for your trust in our work. If you find a moment, we'd love to hear your thoughts and reflections on the book. Your feedback is invaluable to us.

Once again, thank you for being a part of our literary community. *Happy reading!*

Best regards,

The Sport Haven

The Sport Haven

The Antoine Dupont Story

Table of Contents

Early Life and Family Background 4

Rugby Beginnings 9

Rise to Prominence 14

Joining Toulouse 19

National Team Debut 24

Key Matches and Moments 29

Leadership and Style of Play 33

Challenges and Overcoming Adversity 37

Off the Field 41

Legacy and Influence in Rugby 45

The Sport Haven

The Antoine Dupont Story

The Sport Haven

The Antoine Dupont Story

Early Life and Family Background

Born on November 15, 1996, in the quaint village of Castelnau-Magnoac, nestled in the picturesque foothills of the Pyrenees in southwestern France, Antoine Dupont embarked on a journey that would lead him to become one of rugby's most celebrated figures. His early years in the rural heartland of France, where community and camaraderie are deeply valued, set the stage for a life driven by passion, teamwork, and a relentless pursuit of excellence.

Dupont's family, deeply rooted in the region, played a pivotal role in shaping his character and values. His father, a fervent rugby enthusiast, introduced Antoine to the game at a tender age. The sport was not just a pastime in the Dupont household; it was a way of life, a bond

The Antoine Dupont Story

that connected the family and their community. His mother, a constant source of support and encouragement, instilled in him the virtues of humility and hard work, qualities that would later define his approach to both life and rugby.

Growing up in the rural settings of Gers, a department known for its rich rugby tradition, young Dupont was immersed in an environment where rugby was more than just a sport; it was a cultural institution. It was here, in the rugged fields of his hometown club, that Dupont first honed his skills, his natural talent evident from an early age. His innate understanding of the game, combined with a fearless approach to physical challenges, quickly set him apart from his peers.

Despite his burgeoning talent, Dupont's early years were not without challenges. The absence of big-city facilities

The Sport Haven

The Antoine Dupont Story

and resources meant that he had to rely on sheer determination and hard work to refine his skills. Yet, these limitations only served to fuel his ambition. Dupont's parents, recognizing their son's potential, made countless sacrifices to support his budding rugby career. They traveled long distances to take him to training sessions and matches, often juggling work commitments and financial constraints.

As Dupont progressed through his teenage years, his reputation as a promising young talent began to grow. Coaches and scouts from across the region were captivated by his ability to read the game, his quick decision-making, and his fearless tackling. Despite his modest stature, Dupont's strength and agility allowed him to outmaneuver opponents with ease, a trait that would become a hallmark of his playing style.

The Sport Haven

The Antoine Dupont Story

Education, too, played a crucial role in Dupont's development. Balancing academics and rugby, he demonstrated a remarkable ability to excel in both arenas. Teachers and coaches alike praised his discipline and commitment, qualities that transcended the rugby field and classroom. Dupont's formative years were not just about developing his physical skills; they were about cultivating a mindset – one that embraced challenges, valued teamwork, and strived for excellence in every endeavor.

Dupont's transition from a local talent to a rising star in the regional rugby scene was seamless. His performances for his club caught the attention of larger clubs and eventually led to opportunities to play at higher levels. Each step of the way, Dupont remained grounded, a testament to his upbringing and the values instilled in him by his family and community.

The Sport Haven

The Antoine Dupont Story

The influence of his hometown and family cannot be overstated in Dupont's journey. The sense of belonging, the support of a tight-knit community, and the lessons learned on and off the rugby field in Castelnau-Magnoac were instrumental in shaping the player and person he would become. As he stood on the brink of a professional career, Antoine Dupont carried with him not just the hopes of his family, but also the pride of a community that had nurtured one of rugby's brightest talents.

The Sport Haven

The Antoine Dupont Story

Rugby Beginnings

As a child, Dupont's introduction to rugby was almost preordained, given his family's deep-rooted love for the game. His father, an ardent rugby fan, was instrumental in introducing Antoine to the sport. It was under his father's guidance and the watchful eyes of local coaches that Dupont began to learn the fundamentals of rugby, absorbing the skills and strategies that would later define his playing style.

The local rugby club in Castelnau-Magnoac became Dupont's first proving ground. Here, amidst peers and mentors, he began to hone his craft. The club, though modest in its facilities, was rich in camaraderie and spirit. It was in this nurturing environment that Dupont's natural talent began to flourish. His agility, speed, and uncanny ability to read the game set him apart from an

The Sport Haven

The Antoine Dupont Story

early age. He quickly became a standout player, his performances catching the eye of coaches and spectators alike.

Dupont's commitment to rugby was unwavering. He spent countless hours practicing, often extending his training sessions long after his teammates had left the field. His relentless pursuit of improvement was evident in every aspect of his game, from his tactical understanding to his physical conditioning. Dupont's early coaches recall his extraordinary work ethic, a trait that would become a cornerstone of his career.

As Dupont grew older, his skills continued to evolve. He developed a reputation as a dynamic scrum-half, a position that demands quick thinking, strategic vision, and physical resilience. His ability to orchestrate the flow of the game, combined with his fearless approach to

The Antoine Dupont Story

physical confrontation, made him an invaluable asset to his team.

Dupont's talent did not go unnoticed. By his mid-teens, he had caught the attention of scouts from larger clubs. His performances in regional tournaments and youth leagues were a showcase of his burgeoning abilities. In these competitive settings, Dupont demonstrated not just skill, but leadership and poise beyond his years.

The transition from local rugby to a more competitive level was a significant step in Dupont's journey. It presented new challenges and opportunities for growth. Moving to a larger club meant adapting to a higher level of play, facing tougher opponents, and integrating into a new team dynamic. Dupont embraced these challenges with characteristic determination, viewing each obstacle as an opportunity to learn and improve.

The Sport Haven

The Antoine Dupont Story

His move to a more prominent club marked a turning point in his career. It was here that Dupont began to receive formal, structured training, which further refined his technical skills and tactical understanding. The exposure to advanced coaching methods and the opportunity to train alongside highly skilled players accelerated his development. Dupont's adaptability and eagerness to learn were key factors in his rapid progression through the ranks of youth rugby.

As he continued to excel on the field, Dupont's ambitions grew. He set his sights on playing professionally, a goal that seemed increasingly attainable with each passing game. His performances in youth leagues and regional competitions were not just about winning; they were about proving to himself and others that he had the talent and determination to succeed at the highest level.

The Sport Haven

The Antoine Dupont Story

Off the field, Dupont remained grounded and focused. He understood the importance of balancing rugby with his academic pursuits, a discipline instilled in him by his family. This balance helped him maintain a sense of perspective, ensuring that his identity was not solely defined by his success on the rugby field.

The Sport Haven

The Antoine Dupont Story

Rise to Prominence

Dupont's transition from local rugby to playing at a more competitive level was a crucial phase in his development. Joining a larger club offered him the opportunity to train under experienced coaches and compete against top-tier youth players. This move was a significant stepping stone, as it exposed Dupont to a higher standard of rugby, challenging him to elevate his game. His adaptability and eagerness to learn were instrumental in his swift adaptation to the more demanding environment.

During this period, Dupont's natural talent and hard work began to pay dividends. He rapidly became a standout player in his new team, impressing both coaches and teammates with his skill, tactical intelligence, and leadership on the field. His

The Sport Haven

The Antoine Dupont Story

performances in youth leagues and regional tournaments showcased his ability to influence games, whether through his sharp decision-making, deft ball-handling, or tenacious defense.

Dupont's reputation as a rising star in the rugby world was further bolstered by his performances in national youth championships and tournaments. Here, he competed against the best young talent in the country, demonstrating his prowess and earning recognition at the national level. These competitions were not just platforms for showcasing his skills but also valuable learning experiences, exposing him to different playing styles and strategies.

As Dupont's skills continued to develop, so did his understanding of the game. He became known for his ability to read the play, anticipate the opposition's

The Sport Haven

The Antoine Dupont Story

moves, and adapt his style to the demands of each match. This rugby intelligence, coupled with his physical attributes, made him a versatile and formidable player, capable of turning the tide of a game.

The defining moment in Dupont's rise to prominence came with his selection for the France national under-20 team. This was a significant milestone, as it marked his entry into the international rugby arena. Representing his country at this level was both an honor and a testament to his hard work and talent. The experience of playing in international youth tournaments further honed his skills and gave him a taste of rugby at the highest level.

Dupont's performance in the under-20 team was nothing short of remarkable. He played a key role in the team's successes, earning accolades for his contributions on the field. His ability to perform under pressure, combined with his leadership qualities, made him an integral part of the team. This experience not only raised his profile in the rugby community but also bolstered his confidence, reaffirming his belief in his ability to compete at the highest level.

The culmination of Dupont's rise through the ranks came with his transition to professional rugby. His signing with a top-tier club was a dream come true and a validation of his years of hard work and dedication. Stepping onto the professional stage, Dupont was faced with new challenges, including adapting to the intensity and physicality of professional rugby. However, his journey thus far had prepared him well for this leap.

In his debut season as a professional player, Dupont quickly made his mark. He impressed both fans and

The Antoine Dupont Story

critics with his performances, showing that he belonged at this level. His ability to seamlessly integrate into the team and make a significant impact from the outset was a clear indication of his talent and potential.

The Antoine Dupont Story

Joining Toulouse

Dupont's arrival at Toulouse was met with great anticipation. The club, renowned for its commitment to nurturing talent and its rich rugby heritage, was an ideal platform for Dupont to showcase his skills at a higher level. Joining such an esteemed team, however, also meant facing heightened expectations and the pressure of performing on a bigger stage. Dupont approached this new phase of his career with his characteristic blend of humility and confidence, ready to prove his worth in the elite echelons of rugby.

From the outset, Dupont's impact on the team was palpable. His debut season was marked by a series of impressive performances, quickly endearing him to the Toulouse fans and earning the respect of his teammates and coaches. His ability to adapt to the team's playing

The Sport Haven

style and the demands of top-tier rugby was a testament to his skill and work ethic. Dupont's presence on the field brought a new dynamism to the team's play, his sharp instincts and playmaking abilities proving to be invaluable assets.

One of the key aspects of Dupont's time at Toulouse was his development under the tutelage of experienced coaches and alongside seasoned players. This environment provided him with an opportunity to refine his skills further and to learn from some of the best in the game. The high-performance culture at Toulouse, coupled with the club's competitive spirit, pushed Dupont to elevate his game to new heights.

Dupont's role in Toulouse's successes during this period cannot be overstated. He played a crucial part in many of the team's victories, often turning the tide of matches

The Antoine Dupont Story

with his individual brilliance. His performances were not only about scoring tries or making decisive passes; they were also characterized by his relentless work rate, defensive prowess, and ability to inspire his teammates.

The challenges Dupont faced at Toulouse were manifold. Adapting to the physicality and pace of top-level club rugby, handling the expectations that come with playing for a prestigious club, and maintaining consistency in performance were all part of his journey at Toulouse. Dupont met these challenges head-on, displaying a maturity and resilience that belied his age.

His growth as a player during his time at Toulouse was complemented by his development off the field. The move to a new city and a new club environment required adjustments, both personally and professionally. Dupont embraced these changes, showing a willingness

The Antoine Dupont Story

to learn and adapt not only as a player but also as a person. This adaptability and openness to new experiences were key factors in his successful integration into the club and the city.

Dupont's contributions to Toulouse went beyond his individual performances. He became an integral part of the team's identity, embodying the club's ethos of hard work, determination, and excellence. His rapport with teammates and coaches, coupled with his leadership qualities, further solidified his position as a key player in the team.

Throughout his time at Toulouse, Dupont's performances continued to earn him accolades and recognition. He was not just a rising star in French rugby; he was rapidly becoming one of the most talked-about players in the international rugby scene. His journey at Toulouse was

The Antoine Dupont Story

shaping him into a player of exceptional caliber, capable of influencing games at the highest level.

The experience of playing for Toulouse also provided Dupont with valuable lessons in handling success and setbacks. The highs of victories and titles, as well as the lows of defeats and injuries, were all part of the learning curve. Through these experiences, Dupont developed a deeper understanding of the game, a more nuanced approach to his play, and a resilience that would serve him well in the years to come.

The Antoine Dupont Story

National Team Debut

The call to join the French national team came as a recognition of Dupont's exceptional performances at the club level. His consistent display of skill, intelligence, and leadership on the field had caught the attention of national selectors, who saw in him the potential to be a key player for Les Bleus. For Dupont, representing his country was an honor and a responsibility he was eager to embrace.

Dupont's integration into the national team was a momentous occasion, not only for him but also for the rugby community in France. His selection was seen as a testament to the strength of French rugby and its ability to produce world-class talent. As he donned the iconic blue jersey, Dupont carried with him the hopes and expectations of a nation passionate about the sport.

The Sport Haven

The Antoine Dupont Story

The anticipation leading up to his debut was palpable. Fans and pundits alike were eager to see how Dupont would translate his club form onto the international stage. The pressure of representing one's country can be immense, but Dupont approached this challenge with the same determination and focus that had defined his career thus far.

Dupont's debut match was a display of his rugby prowess. From the first whistle, he showcased the qualities that had made him a standout player – his agility, tactical acumen, and ability to read the game. He demonstrated a maturity beyond his years, handling the pressure of the international stage with composure and confidence.

One of the defining aspects of Dupont's national team debut was his ability to adapt to the different playing

The Sport Haven

The Antoine Dupont Story

style and strategy of international rugby. The pace and intensity of the game at this level required a higher degree of physical and mental fortitude, something Dupont possessed in abundance. His performance in his first match was a clear indication that he was not just capable of competing at this level but also of making a significant impact.

Dupont's integration into the national team was further facilitated by his rapport with teammates and coaches. His willingness to learn, combined with his humble yet confident demeanor, endeared him to the squad. He quickly became a valued member of the team, contributing not just through his individual performances but also through his ability to enhance the overall dynamics of the team.

The Sport Haven

The Antoine Dupont Story

The early stages of Dupont's international career were marked by a series of impressive performances. He proved to be a versatile player, capable of adapting his game to suit the team's needs and the specific challenges posed by different opponents. His ability to deliver under pressure, whether in crucial moments of a match or in high-stakes tournaments, was a testament to his character and skill.

Dupont's impact on the French national team was not limited to his on-field contributions. He brought a fresh energy and a new dimension to the team's play. His dynamic style, coupled with his strategic understanding of the game, added depth to the team's attacking options and bolstered its defensive capabilities.

The experience of playing international rugby also provided Dupont with an opportunity for further growth

The Antoine Dupont Story

and development. Competing against some of the best players in the world, in some of the most iconic rugby venues, was both a challenge and a privilege. These experiences honed his skills, broadened his perspective, and reinforced his status as one of the top players in the sport.

The Sport Haven

Key Matches and Moments

One of the early defining moments in Dupont's career came during his time with Toulouse. In a crucial match that would determine the team's progression in a major tournament, Dupont delivered a performance that was nothing short of spectacular. His ability to control the game from the scrum-half position, combined with his tactical acumen and physical prowess, was instrumental in securing a victory for his team. This game was a turning point, solidifying his status as a key player for Toulouse and a rising star in the rugby world.

Dupont's impact was not limited to club rugby. His debut for the French national team was another landmark moment in his career. Stepping onto the international stage, he showcased his readiness to compete at the highest level. His performance in this match was a blend

The Antoine Dupont Story

of skill, composure, and intensity, setting the tone for his future contributions to the national team.

One of Dupont's most memorable moments came in a fiercely contested international match against a traditional rugby powerhouse. In a game that was a true test of skill and character, Dupont rose to the occasion, displaying a masterclass in rugby excellence. His ability to break through defenses, create opportunities for his teammates, and make crucial tackles was central to his team's performance. This match was a clear demonstration of Dupont's ability to influence the outcome of high-stakes games, further enhancing his reputation as one of the best players in the sport.

Another key moment in Dupont's career was his role in a historic victory for France in a major international tournament. His leadership and performance throughout

The Antoine Dupont Story

the tournament were pivotal in guiding his team to success. In the final match, Dupont's strategic play, coupled with his physical and mental resilience, were crucial in securing the victory. This triumph not only brought glory to his team but also cemented Dupont's place as a key figure in French rugby history.

Dupont's journey is also marked by moments of individual brilliance, where his skill and ingenuity were on full display. One such instance was a match where he single-handedly turned the game around with a moment of magic. His extraordinary ability to read the game, combined with his agility and speed, allowed him to execute a play that would be talked about for years to come. This moment highlighted Dupont's unique talent and his capacity to inspire both his teammates and rugby fans.

The Sport Haven

The Antoine Dupont Story

Dupont's career has not been without its challenges. Injuries and setbacks have been part of his journey, yet his response to these challenges has been exemplary. In a particularly difficult period, Dupont demonstrated remarkable resilience and determination to return to the field stronger and more motivated. His comeback match, following a significant injury, was a testament to his character and dedication to the sport. His performance in this game, against all odds, was a powerful reminder of his quality as a player and his unyielding spirit.

Beyond the field, Dupont's influence extends to key moments off the pitch. His commitment to training, his approach to preparation, and his leadership within the team have been integral to his success. Dupont's ability to inspire his teammates, to maintain high standards of professionalism, and to contribute positively to the team's dynamics are as important as his on-field achievements.

The Sport Haven

The Antoine Dupont Story

Leadership and Style of Play

Dupont's style of play is characterized by a unique combination of agility, speed, and tactical intelligence. As a scrum-half, he is the linchpin between the forwards and backs, a role that requires quick decision-making and an ability to read the game. Dupont excels in this regard, consistently demonstrating an acute understanding of the dynamics of rugby. His ability to anticipate the opposition's moves and react swiftly makes him a formidable opponent on the field.

One of the hallmarks of Dupont's play is his exceptional passing ability. His precision and timing in delivering the ball are crucial in setting up attacking opportunities for his team. Dupont's passes are not just functional; they are often creative, opening up spaces and creating angles that

The Sport Haven

The Antoine Dupont Story

disrupt defensive lines. This aspect of his game has been instrumental in many of his team's successful offensive plays.

Another key attribute of Dupont's style is his running game. His agility and acceleration allow him to exploit gaps in the opposition's defense, often leading to significant territorial gains or tries. Dupont's fearlessness in taking on defenders and his ability to stay on his feet in contact situations make him a constant threat on the field. His running game is not just about individual brilliance; it is also a reflection of his understanding of when to exploit opportunities and when to play for the team.

Dupont's defensive capabilities are equally impressive. He is a tenacious defender, known for his commitment and effectiveness in tackling. Despite not being the

The Antoine Dupont Story

biggest player on the field, Dupont's technique and timing in defense make him a formidable presence. His willingness to put his body on the line for the team exemplifies his commitment to the collective effort.

Beyond his technical abilities, Dupont's leadership on the field is a critical component of his style of play. He leads by example, setting high standards for himself and his teammates. Dupont's presence on the field is inspiring; he exudes confidence and a winning mentality that is infectious. His ability to motivate his teammates, maintain focus under pressure, and make critical decisions in the heat of the moment are qualities that distinguish him as a leader.

Dupont's leadership extends beyond the visible aspects of the game. He is a key figure in the team's strategy discussions, contributing insights and ideas that shape

The Sport Haven

The Antoine Dupont Story

the team's approach to matches. His understanding of the game and his ability to communicate effectively with coaches and teammates make him an invaluable asset in planning and execution.

Dupont's style of play and leadership are also reflective of his personality off the field. He is known for his humility, work ethic, and professionalism. These qualities have endeared him to teammates, coaches, and fans alike. Dupont's approach to the game is a blend of passion, intelligence, and respect for the sport and its values.

The impact of Dupont's style of play and leadership can be seen in the successes of his teams at both club and international levels. He has been a catalyst for change, bringing a fresh perspective and a new level of dynamism to the teams he has been a part of. His influence has extended beyond the confines of the rugby

The Antoine Dupont Story

field, inspiring a generation of young players and contributing to the evolution of the sport.

Challenges and Overcoming Adversity

Injuries are an inescapable reality for any athlete, and Dupont has had his fair share. His encounters with injuries have been defining moments, challenging not just his physical capabilities but also his mental fortitude. One such instance occurred early in his professional career, a crucial period in his development as a player. A significant injury threatened to sideline him for an extended period, casting a shadow over his promising trajectory. The prospect of long-term rehabilitation and the uncertainty of returning to peak form were daunting challenges.

The Antoine Dupont Story

Dupont's response to this adversity was a testament to his character. Rather than succumbing to frustration or doubt, he approached his recovery with determination and focus. His rehabilitation process was not just about physical healing; it was also a period of mental and emotional growth. Dupont's commitment to regaining his fitness and form was unwavering. He adhered to a rigorous rehabilitation regimen, worked closely with medical and fitness professionals, and remained positively engaged with his team and the sport.

The journey back to the rugby field was arduous, filled with setbacks and challenges. However, Dupont's resilience in the face of these obstacles was remarkable. His return to the field, post-injury, was a moment of triumph, not just for him but for all who had supported him through his recovery. His comeback game was a display of not just his skill but also his renewed vigor and The Sport Haven

The Antoine Dupont Story

passion for the game. This experience of overcoming a significant injury not only reaffirmed Dupont's physical abilities but also reinforced his mental toughness.

Beyond physical injuries, Dupont has faced other challenges in his career. The pressure of performing consistently at a high level, particularly in the highly competitive and scrutinizing environment of professional rugby, is a constant challenge. Dupont's ability to handle this pressure, to remain focused and composed, is a key aspect of his success. He has demonstrated time and again his capacity to deliver under the most demanding circumstances, whether in crucial matches for his club or in high-stakes international tournaments.

Dupont's journey has also involved adapting to different teams, coaches, and playing styles. Each transition has required him to adjust and integrate into new systems

The Antoine Dupont Story

and dynamics. These changes, while challenging, have also been opportunities for Dupont to grow as a player and a leader. His adaptability and openness to learning have been crucial in navigating these transitions successfully.

Another aspect of the challenges Dupont has faced pertains to the expectations placed upon him, both as an individual player and as a representative of his team and country. The weight of these expectations can be immense, yet Dupont has managed to balance them with grace and professionalism. His approach to the game, characterized by a relentless pursuit of excellence and a team-first mentality, has helped him navigate the pressures of high expectations.

Dupont's journey of overcoming adversity is not just about the challenges he has faced but also about the support system that has been instrumental in his journey. His family, teammates, coaches, and medical staff have played vital roles in his recovery and development. The solidarity and encouragement he has received from this support network have been crucial in his ability to overcome obstacles.

The Antoine Dupont Story

Off the Field

Away from the roaring crowds and the adrenaline of match days, Antoine Dupont's life off the rugby field is a tapestry of personal interests, community involvement, and a grounded lifestyle that contrasts with his on-field persona.

Dupont's roots in the small village of Castelnau-Magnoac have played a significant role in shaping his character. Growing up in a close-knit community, where values like humility, hard work, and solidarity are deeply ingrained, has influenced Dupont's approach to life. Despite his rise to rugby stardom, he has remained grounded and connected to his origins. This connection to his roots is evident in the way he conducts himself off the field, maintaining a simplicity and authenticity that endear him to those around him.

The Sport Haven

The Antoine Dupont Story

One of the defining aspects of Dupont's life off the field is his commitment to his family and close friends. His family, having been a pillar of support throughout his journey, remains central to his life. Dupont often speaks of the influence his family has had on his career and the importance of maintaining strong family ties. His dedication to his loved ones is a testament to his character, highlighting the balance he maintains between his professional and personal life.

Away from rugby, Dupont's interests are diverse and reflect his multifaceted personality. He is known for his love of the outdoors, often spending time in nature, whether hiking, cycling, or simply enjoying the scenic beauty of his native French countryside. These activities not only provide him with a respite from the rigors of professional rugby but also allow him to reconnect with his roots and maintain a sense of balance in his life.

The Sport Haven

The Antoine Dupont Story

Dupont's involvement in community and charitable activities is another significant aspect of his life off the field. He is actively engaged in various initiatives aimed at giving back to the community and supporting causes close to his heart. Whether participating in charity events, supporting youth development programs, or lending his voice to social causes, Dupont's contributions reflect his sense of social responsibility and his desire to make a positive impact beyond the rugby field.

Another interesting facet of Dupont's off-field life is his interest in continuous learning and personal development. He has spoken about the importance of education and the value of acquiring new knowledge and skills. This commitment to learning extends to various areas, from honing his language skills to exploring subjects unrelated to rugby. Dupont's pursuit of knowledge and self-improvement is a reflection of his

The Sport Haven

The Antoine Dupont Story

curious mind and his understanding of the importance of personal growth.

Dupont's approach to health and well-being is also noteworthy. Recognizing the demands of professional rugby, he places a high emphasis on maintaining his physical and mental well-being. His regimen includes not just rigorous training and nutrition but also practices that promote mental health and relaxation. Dupont's holistic approach to health is integral to his performance on the field and his quality of life off it.

In addition to these aspects, Dupont's off-field life is characterized by a sense of privacy and discretion. While he is a public figure, he maintains a low profile when it comes to his personal life, choosing to keep certain aspects away from the public eye. This discretion is a reflection of his humble nature and his respect for the boundaries between his professional and personal worlds.

The Sport Haven

The Antoine Dupont Story

The Sport Haven

The Antoine Dupont Story

Legacy and Influence in Rugby

As Antoine Dupont continues to etch his name into the annals of rugby history, his legacy extends far beyond the accolades and records. Dupont's influence on the sport is multifaceted, embodying his exceptional skills, his distinctive style of play, and his profound impact on teams and fans alike.

Dupont's legacy is first and foremost defined by his remarkable skill set and achievements on the field. His technical prowess, tactical intelligence, and leadership qualities have set new standards in the scrum-half position. Dupont has redefined what it means to be a modern scrum-half, blending traditional responsibilities with a dynamic style that has become a blueprint for aspiring players. His ability to influence games, whether through decisive passes, strategic playmaking, or

The Antoine Dupont Story

defensive tenacity, has made him a standout player in international rugby.

Beyond his individual achievements, Dupont's impact on the teams he has represented is profound. At both club and national levels, he has been a key figure in driving success and fostering a culture of excellence. Dupont's contributions to Toulouse and the French national team have been instrumental in their achievements, elevating the teams' performances in domestic and international competitions. His presence has brought a new level of dynamism and creativity, enhancing the overall quality of play and inspiring his teammates to elevate their game.

Dupont's influence extends to the tactical evolution of rugby. His style of play, characterized by quick decision-making, agility, and a strong defensive mindset, has

The Antoine Dupont Story

influenced the way the scrum-half role is perceived and played. Coaches and analysts often cite Dupont as an example of the modern rugby player, one who combines physical attributes with mental acuity and strategic understanding. His approach to the game has encouraged a rethinking of strategies and tactics, impacting how teams across the world approach their gameplay.

The legacy Dupont is building also resonates with rugby fans and the broader sporting community. His flair on the field, coupled with his humility and sportsmanship off it, has endeared him to fans around the globe. Dupont's journey from a small village in France to the pinnacle of international rugby is an inspiring tale of dedication, hard work, and passion. His story resonates with young athletes, encouraging them to pursue their dreams regardless of their background or circumstances.

The Sport Haven

The Antoine Dupont Story

Dupont's influence is also evident in his role as an ambassador for the sport. His conduct on and off the field exemplifies the values of rugby – respect, teamwork, and integrity. Dupont's commitment to these values and his engagement with fans, especially younger audiences, have made him a role model for aspiring rugby players. His involvement in various initiatives and programs aimed at promoting the sport and supporting youth development further underscores his commitment to nurturing the next generation of rugby talent.

Moreover, Dupont's legacy is marked by his ability to transcend national and cultural boundaries. In a sport that prides itself on international camaraderie and respect, Dupont has become a figure admired and respected by players and fans across different nations. His performances in international tournaments have not only showcased his talent but also fostered a sense of

The Antoine Dupont Story

global rugby community, bringing people together in appreciation of the sport's beauty and spirit.

The Sport Haven

The Antoine Dupont Story

Dear Esteemed Rugby Fan,

Thank you so much for your recent purchase of the book. I do hope you have been able to learn a few or two about your favorite Rugby star. Your support means the world to us, and we're thrilled to have you here. We hope that the pages within provide you with inspiration, creativity and knowledge to being the best at whatsoever athletic endeavor you chose to delve into.

As sports enthusiasts, your enthusiasm fuels our passion, and we are genuinely grateful for your trust in our work. If you find a moment, we'd love to hear your thoughts and reflections on the book. Your feedback is invaluable to us.

Once again, thank you for being a part of our literary community. *Happy reading!*

Best regards,

The Sport Haven

The Sport Haven

Printed in Great Britain
by Amazon